How Can I Say It Was Not Enough?

Anne Kaier

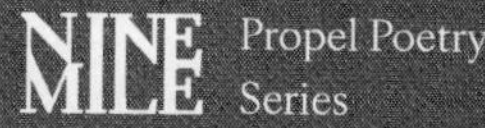

NINE MILE BOOKS:
The Propel Poetry Series

Editors: Stephen Kuusisto, David Weiss
Design Editor: Joshua Unikel
Book and Cover Design: Zoe Collins

Nine Mile Books is an imprint of Nine Mile Art Corp.

ISBN: 979-8-9925462-1-7

Cataloging-in-Publication Data is available upon request.

The publishers gratefully acknowledge support of the New York State Council on the Arts with the support of the Governor and the New York State Legislature. We also acknowledge support of the County of Onondaga and CNY Arts through the Tier Three Project Support Grant Program. This project is made possible with a General Support/Tier Three Project Support grant from the County of Onondaga, with the support of County Executive Ryan McMahon and the Onondaga County Legislature, administered by CNY Arts.

And an especial heart-felt shout-out to the Propel Foundation.

Foreword

Anne Kaier's "How Can I Say it Was Not Enough?" is a generous book. Let's say for argument's sake that poetry readers are, even in the twenty-first century eager to find community on the page. What does that desire "require" if it's to be realized? One thinks of Mary Oliver's "Instructions for living a life": *Pay attention. / Be astonished. / Tell about it.* To this I'll add, invite us in. Kaier is a welcoming poet though the invitation can be quite sober. Consider the poem "Collodion Baby":

> I shrank from my own skin for years,
> withdrawing like a wave that leaves a yellow foam behind.
> But my body waited for me all this time,
> till now at last I reach for kisses
> like the naked baby in her crib.

The generosity I'm describing must always remain invitational. If the body is unreliable, if abjection remains a life-long struggle, then the imagination should of necessity suggest something beyond mere confession. Empathetic visions are what's called for in every aspect of life. But disability and childhood memories remain protean and often dark. Still the poet invites us in:

> For weeks, I languished in the ward, where nurses,
> tending war wounded men,
> neglected me. Then my mom came back,
> tucked me in a wicker laundry basket, carried me
> down the great white steps of Allegheny General,
> and nestled me where she could feed me when I cried.
>
> "I tried hard," she says. "I didn't give up." So, giving up had
> crossed her mind.
> Just let the baby die she might have thought. This strange,
> disordered daughter.

> When all is said and done, do facts speak alone? Or do I need to say, "My mother took my life into her hands and brought me home?"

When I think of open-handed poets, I have some favorites: Audre Lorde, Nikki Giovanni, and oddly enough, Robert Bly. Later in his career Bly wrote:

> The donkey we have loved for years may be killed
> And cooked one day while we go on singing.
> So don't write a single poem without gratitude.

Here's Kaier's poem "After the Golden Afternoon":

> After the golden afternoon,
> when the dark came down like a blade,
> a sudden illumination spoke.
>
> Last night, my widowed mother tossed her auburn hair
> as if she were a girl of twenty.
> "Oh, I turned heads," she said. "The boys flocked around."
> She looked at me and smiled. "But I waited
> for your daddy."
>
> Staring at her candlelight, at last I understood
> how her creed had bound me:
> beauty before marriage, but marriage isn't everything.
>
> What labor, this autumn, readied me
> for this simple truth,
> let it sit upon my mind
> like evening sun on ploughed fields?

These poems demand that we remain open, receptive to the delicate wisdoms of forgiveness. They are not simple truths but that's one of the habits of generosity, or as Robert Frost would say, "you come too."

Anne Kaier is a poet who will not let others tell her story. This is why these poems are so original. And it's why you will be rewarded when reading for they answer the questions about labor and living in both the body and the psyche. She tells us what the work is for. We may call this "disability gain" — a term that's popular within disability communities, the suggestion that the intellect and imagination bring rewards to those with disabilities who think hard. I prefer to conceive of this knowledge as something a bit more complex. Think of William Carlos Williams *The Red Wheelbarrow*. We're told "so much depends" on the sight of rain and chickens but the poet leaves out the critical information behind the poem — a child has died. It is, for all its imagistic virtues not a generous poem. Anne Kaier tells us why the images matter, even to you and I.

Stephen Kuusisto
Editor
The Propel Poetry Series

Skin

Mother Love

Family Clutch

Lovers

Death Songs

Skin

Skin

Tight as tree bark,
skin stretches across my cheek,
pulling provident flesh
down from my eyes,
leaving them bare as winter birch.

In the summer city heat,
my red face gleams.
On my thighs, skin shards rise in ridges,
row after row, sharp as cactus thorn.

Charlie, then five,
fondled my arm, "Don't worry, Auntie,
you'll grow fur."
Only I haven't.

No balm but a stinging salve,
made by a doc in his lab,
or a drug so strong
it eats my bones.

I sit beside my garden yew,
stroke its flanks.
My legs peel in grainy strips,
exposing raw pulp,
leaving thumbs of thick
adhering bark behind.

I bristle;
bound by scale
I cannot burst.

Portrait

The child, naked in her underpants,
stands beneath neon lights
against a white backdrop
down in the hospital basement.
The doctors' photographer
asks if she's cold.
        "No, no. I'm OK."
She looks front and center,
sensing an inch of light beneath
the drawn window shade.
He shoots the fissures in her feet,
her skintight arms.
        "Turn your back toward me, thus."
She spins slowly, as if he were fitting a dress.

Praying

In 1957, when I was eleven, my family and I visited Lourdes, France, where the Virgin Mother was said to have appeared to a local girl in 1858. It became a place of miraculous healing, visited by pilgrims.

We pray for a quick transformation, for a light
switched on in a silent room,
like the aura in the grotto when
the blue Madonna came to bring
instant healing to the sick
who knelt there with a sainted child called Bernadette.

We pray for a slow transformation,
like a journey by train from snow-ridden woods,
past stations flashing in the Carolina dark
'til morning when the land lies level
behind sidings filled with pulped wood
and we finally arrive in—oh, Florida,
where breezes thresh the heat.

We pray for an easy transformation,
a miracle; we desire
to genuflect in the grotto as my skin plumps
in a rain of grace.

Collodian Baby

When I was newborn, my mother said,
a tight and shiny sheath constricting me
cracked through to my flesh so I bled
at my mouth and groin and elbows.
As my doctor gently ripped the membrane off
my chest and arms and back,
I screamed with the slow pain of this debriding,
which left me red and moist, my nerves shivering
in the open incubator.

In my dream last night,
I bent over a woman lying on a gurney,
pregnant with my child.
Her burnt face puffed hollow.
"You'll be alright," I whispered.
"I've been in your skin, too."
Is this the truth? Have I at last recalled
my own flayed infant flesh?
Have I freed my body from mute memories–
and does it matter?

I shrank from my own skin for years,
withdrawing like a wave that leaves a yellow foam behind.
But my body waited for me all this time,
'til now at last I reach for kisses
like the naked baby in her crib.

Cossetted

1.
An organdy dress bought to cup flawless cheeks
fills with a baby whose skin lies thick
in plate-like scales.
She's a river creature,
washed like infant Moses
from some muddy mutation,
a gene gone awry in the womb.

I coo and say her eyes are pretty.
She smiles and her smile cuts
the corners of her lips.
I wipe blood from the cracks and never mind
that her dress is stained.
I pick her up as tenderly as any mother.
I tell her she's pretty, and she smiles.

2.
In our seashore town,
anger hits me like a hot, dry wind.
For someone with damaged skin,
it's a cruel place.
Shoals of girls in bikinis
cruise the hard sand.

As a child, playing in the yard,
squinting at my chest,
jumping around the truth of my legs,
words screened my eyes:
No, no, no, that's not me;
there's nothing wrong.
My playmate said, "You were burned."
Was I? I wondered.

3.
Loneliness shrouds this child;
she can't beat it back.
It shades her when she enters
her mother's glittering party
in her rose velvet dress,
scratching her neck.

4.
In my dream, Mother and I share
red wine in a plush room,
while a half-naked child shivers on a hillside,
her buttocks sluiced with rain.
Thinking, *At least she has red wine in her,*
the memory of something warm,
I watch her crawl into a hole.

5.
On a business trip to the flaming South,
I heard my client ask,
"Will you meet my daughter? She has ichthyosis too.
She's twelve, plays alto sax, likes tamales."

When she sat next to me,
I reached past her father's love,
past the beaches of our thickened skin
and furtive glances at our legs,
that looked a bit like snakes,
to clasp and stroke her rippled grosgrain hand.

The Dermatological Society Skin Fair

1.
In the hospital parking lot,
my heart jumped in my throat.
Surely I'd stand out among the "afflicted"
displaying their disorders to a pack of docs roving
from examining room to examining room
at the spring fair.

Perched on white crepe paper, I handed out
my Xeroxed resume as each physician strolled into my space:
"Harvard Ph.D., Home-Owner, Published Poet."
I hoped they'd recognize the real, throbbing me.
For an hour or more, two by two they came, with sharpened
eyes.
Each took my bio, but no one said a word about it.

I thrust my peeling arm in their soft palms.
Each scrutinized it, dropped it, asked: "When did your
condition start?"
"At birth." *Didn't you read my medical chart?*
I took off my wig, bent my torn and scaly scalp beneath
their probing fingers.
"You're the star of the show!" the youngest intern said.
"The only full-body case."
Swinging my fissured legs against the metal table,
I answered all their questions through my teeth.
At least I haven't got a sign that says: "Alligator Girl."
Alone, I fell back, flayed.

2.
That night, a dream woman juts scarred arms,
like knuckled wood, towards me.
I touch her burnt-red hair,
my hands wet, electric.
"Feel my arms," she says. "Feel them."

I cannot finger the ridges where
shard, lash, or knife
slashed her arms.
"Touch my wounds," she says.
I cannot move my moist hands off her head
to stroke her skin and cling there.

Can't Tell

How the skin on my thighs looks like salt;
how the owl's in the linen closet
in the hallway at home.

How fiery trees flash in the late afternoon,
fire in the lane, always fire, fire in the fireplace.
How lonely I am, so core alone, so hard to say it.
Now almost fifty, and no one's chosen me.

Can't tell how I look at guys' crotches in the street,
Thinking, *Let me feel you up, let me have it hard, let me suck it,*
let me, let me, watch it pushing,
knobby under khaki, so attached,
and me watching in the cool side street
on an August afternoon, walking
home to the house empty from bottom to top.

I can tell how I hide in the soft summer night and oh
the brilliance of the early morning light.

Shore Bird

1.
Today, I heard that Joan,
with fish-scale skin like mine,
had normal, happy children.

Oh look, I thought,
I could have gotten pregnant,
but he was full of mania, and I was full of toxins;
the doctor said my babies would have
ears in their foreheads.
Manic-depressive kids with happenstance ears?
I made sure that didn't happen.

2.
Our youngest art director's baby
was due on Christmas Day.
Jesus van Saun, we teased her.
She lifted him, round as a melon in her womb,
and set him on her low desk.
Weary, she prayed for a safe delivery, as mothers do.

In my dream, she sat with her newborn on her lap.
I walked a tightrope
to make my obeisance.

3.
Nothing I can ever do,
nothing,
equals the pure fact of childbirth;
nothing.

I'm a shore bird.
The great currents
merely tongue
my feet.

How My Body Mourns

How my body longs for skin
as satin smooth as a blushing, pink magnolia
or the radiant ivy vines that climb my garden tree.
My body mourns desiccated
molecules that swarm my bones,
stretch the planes of my face.

Ancient genes want out
so that a supple tendril
from the normal mucus of my vulva,
can rise along my thighs and back and breasts,
spread across my flesh,
lick the nerves in my arms so I
can slide into a man's embrace,
coil around his chest,
open to him like a
thick moonflower.

How my body longs for rest from itch, from its own
false, desert dunes.

Saturday Night

In my narrow stairwell,
one stroke on my clit
opens
pastures, prairies, rills
between legs that peel
like birch.

Mother Love

The Dressing Table

In the danger zone of mother's dressing room,
at five on a February day,
I watched her work at her mahogany table,
a slender woman in a slip.
After years as a practicing beauty,
she sketched high brows and blushed her coral cheeks.

I sat in a blue chintz chair,
hardly a gazelle at fifteen.
Her perfume looked like scotch.
With hands that stroke so hard it hurts,
she rubbed on gloss; then smacked
her lips and snapped the compact shut,
as if she'd trumped at cards.

I fed on the scent of her,
willing her to bring me into the game of
women hunting men,
but she kept her secrets to herself.

She stepped into her satin gown.
"Zip me up, will you, honey? I'm late."
My rough, red fingers fumbled
pinning a spray of diamonds at her breast.
She flicked her eyes at her full-length mirror,
"How do I look?"
What could I say? "Gorgeous."
She curved her hand half-moon
around my face and rustled out.

Mother's Perfume

I brought another jar from France
in its brown Art Deco box.
She asked if I had ever smelled it.
        Of course I had. On her dressing table,
        in her hair, on a sweater in her chest of drawers.
"Daddy loved that scent," she said, remembering—what?
A touch, a kiss from her lover,
nearly fifty years ago?

In Church

Hunched against the altar rail,
my naked haunches spread,
I watched the church bloom around me,
a place of pleasure where
light falls on cloth of gold,
on incense motes and ancient chants.
There I sat, riding my thighs,
gardenias in a bowl by my hand,
eager to preach a passion sermon
and rub the fragrant petals to myself,
when mother started from a wooden pew,
a killing prohibition in her eyes.

Mother Love

1. Visiting you
Thin with muscle like twisted rope,
you hugged me tight—a welcoming ritual
you always make at your back door. You smiled,
looked proprietary, as if you knew
you own me deep.

2. At your dinner table
"I could have let you die when you were born," you said,
clawing your goblet of wine.
I settled my buttocks in the back of my chair,
safer in the fullness of my flesh, opening a little
at that candlelit table, where I have lingered, waiting
for you to strike.

We sat in that high, wide room,
windows open to crickets' hum.
Your hands stroked a silver knife, hands
so strong they hurt a baby when you rock it.
Looking at the flame, you said, "I could have let you die of
 your disease;
no one would have blamed me."

But my body, my body, you kept it
from me. You kept it sterile,
high in a serpentine crack
in the ceiling.
It's not my flesh but a thing I wear around
like an unshed snake skin.

3. The waiting room
When Dr. Shelley snapped the curtain shut,
you flirted with him. I always knew
you had a thing for Shelley.

I offered my small arm, a ruler's length of scale,
for his soft, scientific gaze
as you asked, "Anything new, a cure?"

On the ride home, closed in the car,
my body hovered like a fly on the windowpane.
I shriveled further in the skin we
never said a word about.
You begged me, "Talk to me, Anne, talk to me!"

I could not please you,
I could not make my arm,
my twelve peeling inches,
clean, soft, pretty.

4. Thanksgiving
You sat at the head of your table
like a great spider;
there for fifty years,
you've spun a net of linens, flowers, Merlot fumes.

You told Indiana stories,
looking through the great bay windows to the hawthorn tree,
drinking champagne in a Waterford glass.

"When I was young," you said, "the Ku Klux Klan
burnt crosses on our Courthouse lawn.
We saw white hoods in my boyfriend's house, but
we didn't think a thing about it."
"Weren't you afraid?" I asked. "The Klan hated Catholics
in Indiana in the twenties."
"Oh no, no," you said, "no..."
I gave it up, turned to my brother, Ed.
"Why wouldn't she have been afraid?" I asked.
"She was a pretty girl," he said.
"She knew they wouldn't hurt a pretty girl."

Coda

Your kisses have always been wet, Mother;
your mouth open, your mouth on mine, wet with love.
Should I take your body now,
taut with muscle, slender still,
scars where breasts should be;
should I fold you in my arms,
smooth my hands along your pelvic bone,
lick your pubic hair, still black and thick
in my imagination?

You are young there,
there in your inner lips.

My mouth sucks your mound.
I suckle your sexual self,
your lips, your juice.
I wind your black hairs
around my tongue.

If I make love to you at last,
will you let me go?

When All is Said and Done: Mother at Eighty-Five

1.

Her mouth gleams mauve against her face; her smile spreads ferocious.
She sits upright in her languorous backyard chair.

That morning in the summer heat, she'd played the full eighteen, every single hole. "Oh yes, I always play eighteen. It's no good playing nine."

Cradling her scotch, her kitten nosing at her feet, she gives instructions for her china:
"After I die, I want it all to come to you. Your brother can take care of his wife."

2.

We eat our dinner on a terrace at the club, overlooking sand traps – oval scarabs on the Pennsylvania land. I scan the shapes of trees—how they sway in a breeze.

A child in a white dress stares at me, stunned at my red, round face
among the crew-cut Catholics in their peach and green. I stare back,
hard like a cat.

Driving myself home by the river, I hear ancient sycamores swing, crickets sing in the underbrush.

I bend above the steering wheel, shot through with her bullets. "Talk to me," she said. "Your brother doesn't call. Talk to me!"

In my own house, a piece of charcoal lies near a clean white jug.
I lift the stick, slash the sketch book page.

Tonight she told me, tearing up, about her last, real embrace with her man.

"We knew his mind had dimmed. He knew that I'd take care of
him."

Their love thrusts through my belly.

3.

Every time I see her now, she talks about the day that I was
born.
When she woke from ether, Daddy smiled wide. "We have
twins, Pat."
Later, seeing how the baby's brittle skin broke and bled,
he urged his wife, "Talk to her, Pat, talk to her."

For weeks, I languished in the ward, where nurses, tending war
wounded men,
neglected me. Then my mom came back,
tucked me in a wicker laundry basket, carried me
down the great white steps of Allegheny General,
and nestled me where she could feed me when I cried.

"I tried hard," she says. "I didn't give up." So, giving up had
crossed her mind.
Just let the baby die, she might have thought. This strange,
disordered daughter.

When all is said and done, do facts speak alone? Or do I need
to say,
"My mother took my life into her hands and brought me home?"

After the Golden Afternoon

After the golden afternoon,
when the dark came down like a blade,
a sudden illumination spoke.

Last night, my widowed mother tossed her auburn hair
as if she were a girl of twenty.
"Oh, I turned heads," she said. "The boys flocked around."
She looked at me and smiled. "But I waited
for your daddy."

Staring at her candlelight, at last I understood
how her creed had bound me:
beauty before marriage, but marriage isn't everything.

What labor, this autumn, readied me
for this simple truth,
let it sit upon my mind
like evening sun on ploughed fields?

Mothers and Daughters

1.
Last night, I came to her again,
up the tree-lined allée of her love.
She sat in judgment:
"Why are you leaving your corporate job? Don't they like you
now?"
I didn't dodge while she
fixed her gaze on me. "What's your plan?" she asked, snorting.
"Write, read, teach," I answered, looking her full in the eye.
"Come live with me," she said, sensing her chance
to comfort and contort me, tangle
my branches with hers.
"No," I said, "it would never work; you know that."
She shrugged. "The offer's always open."

Perhaps I'm learning how to tell the truth
and still survive it.

2.
Then we spread old photos on the table: an Indiana wedding,
1917.
Her mother and her aunts strolling in her grandfather's garden.
Tonight she laughed and named their names: Grace, Louella,
Josephine.
The bride, Aunt Jo, wore plumes, waltzed in her husband's
arms.

3.
I took a photo home—without permission.
My mother, still a silken child,
curves her arm around her widowed mama's waist.
Nana stands upright. A string of wooden beads falls past her
breasts.
She holds her daughter to her; and in her look, she will kill
anyone who comes too close.

Not me, I swore. *This will never be a snap of mom and me.*
I'm not that kind of daughter.
Still, she and I have sidled near each other lately.
I wouldn't call it courting—
maybe just less wary love.

Old Roses

December 31, 1999
dusk

Today, you called to say how much you love me, Mother.
Suddenly, I saw old roses in your face, roses
like the thick fragrant reds that throng
your silver chastened bowl in summer;
roses like the climbing whites
that grow around your bedroom window;
roses like the yellow cups that circle
some pensive Degas woman.

Oh, let your roses shine tonight
in the last blue light.

My Mother's Voice

My mother's voice won't leave me
when she dies. It twists
cords in my throat,
throttles my song, rings
me out. Inoperable, mine
since I could hear it,
her voice lives in my tones,
twines through my voice,
as mine through hers,
like two vines, their roots in tangled love
commingled.

If I unbind one
from the other, both
will die out.

Family Clutch

Twin

1.

Womb brother, old swimmer,
with me when my skin malformed;
did you know that there was something wrong?
We floated side by side,
you and I, all those months,
bumping each other, unwary dancers.
We never had to be alone with her,
even though she didn't know it.
She didn't know that there were two of us,
putting our heads together.

In the crib, murmuring,
I felt your kindness, Father's gift.
Love sits in the nape of your neck.

2.

I've thought to find the untold story,
the bitter wine of your good fortune—smooth
skin, a woman to warm your Irish chest,
but all I find from fifty years and more,
is stubborn sweetness.

3.

The night your baby girl was born,
I dreamt a lovely dream of making love to you.
In and out, your arms around me,
I claimed you, lost
at birth and claimed again
in Tory's birthing.

4.

I want to write of you in soundings
Yeats might use, you gentle Irish man;
goodness steeped in your arms,
sweet as honey.

Easter

For years, I stayed away or hid
behind my camera,
watching my brother's children run
where we had run
through the waving beeches,
around the hot pine stumps,
searching for hidden eggs.

Do they see it—the gentle fathers and the watching mothers?
Do they see the rushing blood?

When I was a child, this yard was mine,
every ant and firefly,
every crawling worm,
acknowledged me.

But now, no child of mine runs through this grass,
bearing my blood, my birth, my eyes.

At the Paschal table tonight,
my brother made an Easter prayer,
weeping in God's thin light
for the son he lost ten years ago.

We both saw ghosts.

I came this Easter to feel in my own feet
how it hurts to be here, rooted
where I do not bloom,

but through my soles a vision rose:
a child, red-faced, curly-haired,
her arms outstretched, ran
towards me through the empty yard.

"Mother," she called out, "Mother."

The Bride Triumphant

The bride, triumphant in custom's chalice,
holds her lover's trembling hand,
while a joyful Kaier family monk
stands at the altar where
he presided at my brother's wedding
twenty years ago.

Today, I've donned the golden dress
of an observer-poet.
It spares me from my mind's bold stare
at my own unwanted body,
so unfit for rituals such as these.
There's a place for single women
in the Catholic Church;
we come in third, after
nuns and mothers.

The groom's a Protestant;
his people throng the wedding feast.
I grin, greet friend and foe among
the Quaker aristocracy in Oxford shirts and ties.
We all observe the wedding rites: the toasts, the cake, the flung
    bouquet.
Every step's as clear as parquetry.
In the spacious room where ranks of brides
have danced into the codebooks,
that splendid filly, my brother's niece
takes her turn.
I, champagne in hand,
watch myself watching myself
and feel securely foreign to myself.

That night, my body comes to me
as my cunt juice echoes in my bed;
flesh, scaly on the outskirts,
holy as any blessed today,
sings in its own soft mouth.

Seashore Town

Seen behind the gray porch screen,
our strip of sea lies listless, worn.
It shrinks from the dike the crews have built,
in deference to the foaming ocean.

Just to be, just to be, just to hear the sea and the crickets.

Across the street, soldier-proud McMansions stand.
Buzz saws sting the air. But the dunes are back;
their grasses spread from orange mesh,
throw febrile runners through the sand.

Just to be, just to hear the sea and the crickets.

My old friend fed me flounder yesterday.
For fifty years, we've frolicked in this strip of ocean.
We know the currents, where sand bars lie,
how far to swim when the lifeguards have gone.

Just to hear the sea and the crickets.

Today, the ocean's full of foul shell shards.
Dishwater waves rock us. The porch smells plump with mucus.
In the fraught air, I sit suspended.
Then, evening breezes rush along my hair.

Just to hear the sea.

Our neighbor turns ninety today; she spies on teens and tells.
We children used to lie in bed on August nights
and listen to her brood play "Don't Be Cruel."
We'd watch their shadow figures dancing on the wall.

Just to be, just to hear.

Tonight, my friend takes family photos on the beach.
Her grandchildren splash where my nephews splashed.
Twenty years ago, one of the children died
but he emerges in his brother's face.

In this hot place, elders and kids live side by noisy side;
the sea presides—handsome, dirty, kind.

Just to be, just to be, just to hear the sea and the crickets.

When Mother Sells the Family Home

In the legend of the Pelican, the mother bird tears the flesh of her own breast to feed her young in times of famine.

1. Piano man
Yesterday, the knacker, Sweeney,
dragged away my Dad's piano.
He knocked its legs off,
hauled the broken hulk out the Tudor door.

Dad used to play tunes from the '20's
beneath a potted palm.
I curbed my young voice by his side, grateful
for his manly smell, the auburn hair on his hands.
Now and then, I sang a bit,
my big soprano drowned out by his tenor.

Dreaming, I saw the ocean breakers steal
a grand piano; waves obscured the score.
I didn't lift a hand to save it.

2. Pelican
Candles shone along our polished table,
while mother smoothed her linen cloth.
When she leaves, will everything dissolve,
or will the mirror shimmer nights when she
pecked my breast, spurting resentments
she's nourished fifty years and more?
"My father died. We had no money. But my mother—so
  feminine!"
She spat it all into the candlelight;
I bowed to her beak, ducking when the mirror
flashed my face right back at me.

3. Leave-taking
When, after more than sixty years,
mother surrenders our garden,
will my imaginary friends from childhood
linger there within the old pine trees?
Of course not; they'll come with me.

Out behind the bristling tree,
a boy waited for me to sprint.
No! It was the tree,
the tree whose bark matched my scratchy legs.
It was the tree itself who waited there.

Now when the house is gone,
who will my willing arms hold?

It was the tree, felled years ago, who waited.

4. Moving day
Mother came to her old-age home clutching
the last gardenias from her garden,
which every summer hummed with bees.
She'd point her hoses in July
at roses rimmed in Revlon red;
she'd make bouquets for vases in the hall,
where windows opened for the fireflies.

Tonight, the bare house breathed the rain,
the attic stared, emptied of its family relics.
Floorboards hesitated, waiting
for other kids to slide along the hall,
dash beneath the copper beech
onto the virtuous lawn.

She's left, transplanted to a tiny patio
where the wind swings a single pot of petunias.

We prettied up the place with wallpaper posies,
a mirror wide enough to bring the meadow in,
but we knew she'd moved into the last rooms
she'll ever fill with her taut scent.

5. Sitting at the table
Her dining table's come to me,
redeemed from all her angers.
It's come delighted as a girl to hold
my blue and yellow candlesticks,
to serve—a holy place where I can sit to read
and hear the fountain in my garden;
there a woman clothed in water
holds her speckled arms toward me.
I gesture towards her touch.

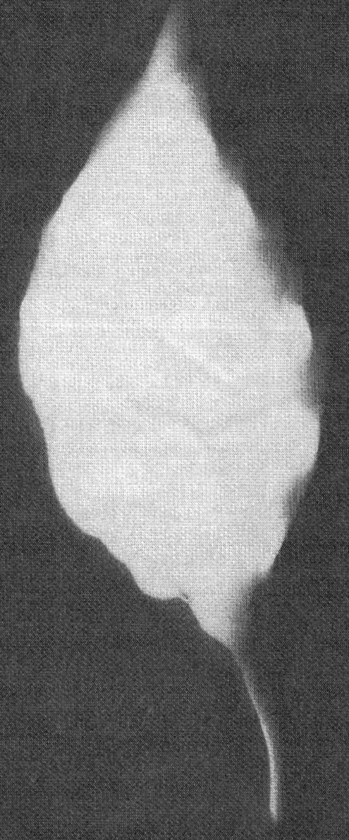

Lovers

Redlight Blue

It's razzmatazz, this spring
thing, this fling in a
wake-up world,
this crazy thing called
love. Love again, oh careless love. Oh love
on earth, in a plane, in a medevac chopper in the clear blue sky.

Hell, it's lunchtime in the city and who
are all these folks walking down
the street? Street meat. Sweetmeats swingin'. A girl with
golden hair. A chick with flair and a guy with grit.
Gritty guy nitwits and purple clowns on stilts.
Then it's longhaired freakies sitting
in the park. With dogs. Feeding the dogs, long dogs, little
dogs, log dogs, riddle dogs, dog dung. In plastic bags.

Now it's the dog hour, the hour of the dog.
Walking, talking, swinging shit. At the blue hour,
l'heure bleue. When the dog walkers go
home with their runts to rut, or whatever. Eat
a meal. Watch the news. Go to bed. Devil the bed.
Red. Said, sad, that ole bed. The sky swings
around and the streetlight stuns the room blue,
redlight blue. All night long.

In the Pink

Childhood scars remember
the fall from the yellow cradle,
a jagged table edge,
spilt coffee burning
a wreath on the baby's wrist.

The sharp scalpel lifted
a cube from my left thigh,
an inch of baby flesh
so they could figure out
what went wrong with my skin in the womb.

The sample gave no answer,
but the scar remained, spreading
its memory of the day
when the knife left a ridge
smooth enough
for my lover's thumb.

Heat

When lilies burst in the sun,
I open to their scent.
Boisterous purple iris flowers
charm my watering eyes.
My ears adore cocky finches,
the crickets' evening swell. But touch

tightens me; nerves that
flicker towards a hand
ignite my skin like wires
sparking down my back.

So what am I to do?
I need a desert lover
to want my orange dunes
and find my wells.

Dock

"You look wonderful," he said
when I, hot from the subway,
appeared again in Harvard Square,
in a red dress, newly cured or semi-cured
with breasts like slightly sandy Bosc pears
instead of thick and bumpy pineapple peel.

He took me to the harbor dock
where he went sailing
in his only pin-striped suit.
Dangling our legs in the water, his pale Irish feet met
my thick-skinned toes, which he forgave
or didn't see, or didn't care, since I was semi-cured.

Back in a rented room, we made love, laughing,
Irish Catholic love—halting, witty, guilt-obscured.
I had a man whom I had known and loved for years,
who Mother warned would never want me,
but now, I loosened to his touch
and, in the morning, lounged in linen shorts,
triumphant as a bride.

She Appeared Again Last Night

She appeared again last night,
the woman in the house.
I
saw her glowing out of shadow,
a femme in a film noir.

She surprised me
in a blurred blue slip,
wide breasts, a sly look,
someone known.

At the bottom of the stairs,
she waited for me,
and when I slowly passed her,
I could not take her hand.

Come Kiss Me Like Oranges

Come kiss me like oranges, kiss me.
Kiss me with your dark unruly hands,
your azure earring falling on my cheek,
your myth in my mouth: come
kiss me.

Come to me slowly,
coax me from stillness,
tense as a totem.

Woo me, woo me, want me,
woo me.

Come to my garden,
kiss me like oranges; kiss me,
your lips rasping my throat,
your tongue circling my breast,
your look in my eye.

Come kiss me like oranges,
kiss me, kiss me.

You Would Understand How

You would understand how,
in the early dark, wanting
to hoard the seagull's scream
against the winter,
I came to the summer house,
disturbed the dust sheets,
made a pool of light with a candle's flame,
and rocked, thinking of your yellow hair,
wanting you so my belly
bent and reared toward your wrist
'til I hid in the old iron bed and
warned you, who were home with your mate,
to step around the tackle on my floor
so your legs wouldn't buckle in the dark,
and how in the thin November morning,
I wandered past sand-loving plants,
climbed the warm and sliding dunes
until, at last, the sea spread out and took you.

A Clutch of Narcissus

On a lark, I stopped by her yellow shop.
Traffic in children's books slacks off in spring,
so I surprised her with a spill of daffodils.
This time, her shoulders leaned toward mine.
Will I find my body by fingering hers?

Later, at home, my thumb slides along
a ridge of skin beneath my jaw to touch her neck,
gray and hard behind her ears.
I stroke her puckish hand, whose knuckles pop,
whose fingers clench beneath themselves.
I rub the curve of her arthritic wrist,
feel the rush of her blood.

Donkeys on Parade

Brides on donkeys ride beside a train.
I'm on the train; it goes faster and faster,
intent on causing a wreck.
On its prow, as on a screen, the faces
of middle-aged men appear.
When the train jumps the track,
the men's faces explode in broken pixels.
The brides, their white gowns muddy and bloodied,
pick their way home.

> Lately, I like young men, one above all.
> I watch the curl at the nape of his neck,
> his hooked look when we read Blake in class.

How soft and kind my body is in morning light
when lazy rivers ripple through its hills.

> Tonight, the moonlight strikes my page.
> I'm reading Revelation,
> full of apparitions St. John met
> on Patmos long ago.

They are welcome, the demons. Welcome.

Haven

for Suzanne

My heart's home
is your quiet spare room
where I sleep
as if safe in your arms.

My feet slide
on the sandy bare floor;
crickets sing,
and the soft sea air
ripples the sheets.

One summer night,
you took me to the Yacht Club ball.
Maybe I was your date
because you, my queen of AA,
needed someone content
with lemonade.

We sat in a cove of the room
while the hard drinking Irish
hung on the bar.
For an hour or so you fed on me,
let me slip in and out of your thoughts
while you blinked your clear, green eyes.

Dancing, you closed again.
Your arms were yours and yours alone.

Do I always come when you call?
Now and then, I chance it.

My reward that night
was to sleep in your simple back room.

How can I say it was not enough?

Debbie: Sunday Night Lover

1.

When your hand stroked my thigh,
warmth deep as pain
stung between my legs,
and my flesh remembered the green bathroom
where my body lay in mother's hands
on summer nights
when she slapped cold cream
on the fissures in my baby skin,
working on a table by the open window,
reading to me while she kneaded,
scouring me like a blackened pot
until I felt the heat beneath her touch.

2.

You waited on my damask bed,
clasping your left hand with your right,
like a soldier at ease.
When you swung towards me,
your breasts moving side by side,
your body shadowed mine.
"Are you afraid?" you asked.
"Do I seem afraid?"
"Yes," you said.
"Should I be afraid of you?"
"No," you said,
but your kiss bit.

Today, you called to tell me
something new had happened;
you awoke this morning, aroused
by the sting
of my tongue.

3.

There you stood, hips ajar,
stiff with anger at me and mine,
until I drove you out
with my silent voice:
Go home, lover, go home, don't pressure me
to take you to my mother's place tomorrow.

I sat and drank a beer,
and soon I saw you in my mother's home,
shifting in your chair,
washed in the shimmering Easter light,
light falling like achieved grace,
light lingering after nightfall
behind the four great windows
of her dining room.
I saw you there, smelling of talcum,
your clean white shirt sloping
the curve of your breast.

But I didn't take you. Instead
I bought a guilt offering:
French soap; thinking,
Nothing I can do will be enough for you,
you who were left in the orphanage
with two parents living.
You will eat me up, I thought.
You will leave me husked.

On Easter day, you called
to offer your forgiveness.
"I'll go to my sister's," you said.

        Suddenly, I saw you wait for me,
        like a nude runner
        rocking on the balls of your feet.

4.

Last night, you lay flat,
an elbow behind your head,
your blue eyes closed,
seeing only frightening scenes
as my tongue flicked your nipple
and my hand breezed your thigh
like a punkah wallah, following instructions;
while now and then, I tried
to suck a kiss from you
by force of will;
my skin, too present in my mind,
kept me taut, my sap and juices caught within.
"Turn on me," I begged you. "Turn
yourself on me," but you lay back
and gripped my bristling fingers in the slime and muscle
of your cunt
while your body filled
with other people's lust:
your husband spat you through my tongue,
your father tore you with my fingers
'til you sat up shaking, and I tried to calm
the curve of your butt
with my empty hand.

5.

Your breasts hung thick
beneath your undershirt
when you bent to kiss
me this morning.

We'd argued all night;
You'd rung me like a heavy gong:
"I won't touch you," you'd said,
"if you run with other women."

But then, this morning,
you burnished my back
with the ritual Reiki massage
you sell to almost anyone
who'll pay your price.

6.

When I think of a healing place,
I see Balinese islands
where twilight rises pink and iris
and I sit in the center of an open room,
shriveled on a teakwood chair,
and then I know again,
the only real comfort comes in your flimsy bed,
when I twist my legs around your legs,
and your supple skin becomes my skin,
and your touch seeps into me. After that,
for half a day, at least,
I am still
beneath your hand.

Speculation

Will I restore my garden's shine,
rim the pool with peacock tile,
turn the fountain on once more,
tempt new women with outworn guile,

or yet again console myself
with fetching, comely foreign girls—
flirt with Renoir's balcony belle,
wink at a Matisse fondling her pearls,

chat with a bronze on an English lawn,
ponder Vita's Persian guise,
or watch a languid Rembrandt nude
brush her scarves on amber thighs?

To the Garden

There's the question of slugs;
they slither down your walls
to rag my antique roses.
Your ancient bricks have sunk
beneath the drains so muddy pools
rim the fountain; yellow spiders
sling their hammocks round your limbs;
the cat manures the fern.

But when I waltz into your evening arms
and smell your fragrant hair,
fondle your lustrous, white moonflower,
then am I loved, safe, caressed.

Madame X

Painter John Singer Sargent's most famous portrait, called Madame X, is of Virginie Gautreau, a celebrated American beauty living in Paris in the 1880s, known for her sexual allure.

I want to be you, Madame X,
I want to walk in your silky pale skin,
stir your black satin dress,
feel men's admiring eyes and the glances women give to
  glamor
as I glide in furs down the Rue di Rivoli.
I want to swing in your cool thighs,
feel my blood pink your breasts,
pulse in your lovely, lucid arms,
I want to clench your inner lips curled in their brown nest,
cohabit you, leave my rough, red skin behind.

Rescue me, Madame X,
take me out of this body not my own,
reach your suave hands toward me,
bring me to you, hip to hip,
reach in and rescue me.

I was born to be a beauty, to all the love that comes with
  loveliness.
Lift me to you, Madame X, wrap your arms around me,
curve your legs with mine.
Reach down and rescue me from stale abandonment,
reach down as if you were the Virgin Mother,
reach down and raise me up.

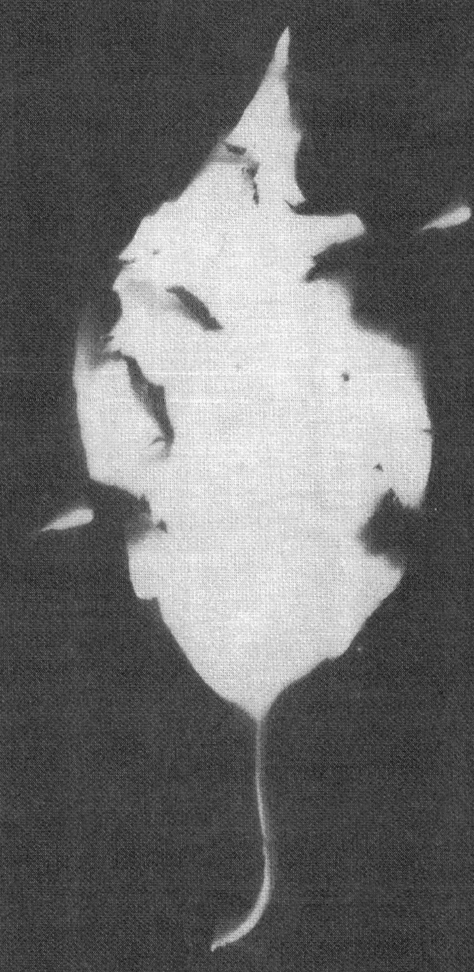

Death Songs

All Souls'

On the Feast of All Souls, prayers are said for the souls of the faithful departed. It's the day after All Saint' Day, reserved for the Church's elite.

On a young November day, I scratch the bottom
of my last batch of raspberry jam
and think to buy in bulk against the coming dark.
How do you hoard against that other winter?

Out back, my orange mums collapse into their pot.
Red yew berries scatter,
birds squawk and fight,
scream and feast.

I sit in the golden garden light while loving souls
come to me; no fanatic
medieval saints with twisted tongues crusading,
no innocent women martyred.

This afternoon, the souls come to comfort and console us.
My father claps his hands to see me.
His namesake, Eddie, dead at four, rocks his
berry-red curls.

My uncle's face comes through, he who winked
on his deathbed.
A brilliant British friend grins, surprised to see me;
my Nana breaks into a cunning smile.

Must I soon be one of them?
Perhaps I'll find that heaven's like my garden
on a warm November afternoon,
luminous, languid, still.

But the souls can't fill my arms. Dear ephemera,
 they open up the spaces in between,
the empty air no souls can cross or maybe only souls can
 cross it—

heatless, fleshless, fleshy souls—spirits with flesh and hot
 blood who leave us
lost in the blue light of evening
 on All Souls' night.

Skull

for Alexandra Grilikhes

1. Forecast
What will your dying be like
there in your lover's bed?
Will you let me touch you
when your face hollows?
Weeks ago, I leant against you on a couch
and pressed my hand in yours
so you will know me
when you're dying.

I saw you in New York at twenty,
slapping a painted drum,
laughing, lifting
your left eyebrow.

Sitting on the purple sofa,
your skull's curve filled my hand;
you bowed your head beneath my stroke.

2. Teacher
Tumors snaked your chest
in her bedroom suffused with your smell.
You threw your gaunt head back,
pulled your starving body up.

Busses groaned on Manayunk Road
that late December afternoon.
Tight-lipped, I sewed beneath a Tiffany lamp,
remembering when

you strode into your kitchen,
twitched your yellow hair, and said,

"Even a woman who has no child,
feels like a mother."

"Even a woman who has no child,
feels like a mother."

I stitched a linen cloth,
ate your face with my eyes.

3. Vigil
I watched Christ's ribs jut
from his polychrome chest
made of twisted wood,
while I circled that Burgundian cross—
its russet limbs, its red cuts,
the only salve that I could stand
those winter days when
you lie dying.

Bending over your lover's bed,
I took your head in my hands,
stroked your spiky hair,
fingered the long line of vertebrae
studding your back,
chose black towels
so you wouldn't see the blood
when it choked your throat.

You died in morphia,
your body finally
empty; I'm told
not to harry your spirit,
to let you go,
but I still feel the brush
of your skull
on my breast.

So Why Do Pain and Fear Buy Heaven?

Maybe Hamlet's right. It's what's unknown,
the undiscovered country, that gives us pause—
even for a young man like Hamlet, who,
though in a very bad fix, has shapely legs,
and a compliant girlfriend.
But he's on to something.

If you are frozen out in some forsaken nursing home,
in bed with a fly, and you can't get up, but
you have a stash of pills—well, the nurses
probably count the pills—yet
if you managed to bury the pills under your pillow, and the fly
who was, after all, free to leave, wouldn't,
would God mind so much,
even having fixed his canon 'gainst self-slaughter,
if you ignored that rule and swallowed them?

Lying there, when nightmares glare
like the seven deadly sins; when they frolic
in the daytime, peering, leering
from the metal table; when they zoom
in the window and swoop across your bed at noon;
when your brain lets loose grotesques in your skull,
gargoyle faces you can neither tame nor know;
when jeering men kept down for years come out
to flog and beat and eat you, you'll want to drown
your sense in odors, float like Ophelia
to a soft and watery death.

A Bouquet for Mother in the Memory Unit

I brought you tulips in your dotage—
and dotage it was, your mind no longer sharp
though a smile spread across your face
when I rambled in; you started up
from your cumbrous wheelchair,
silent, speechless, thrilled to see me.

How could I not adore you then?
Your purest smile, fulfilled with love,
broke upon me and those simple tulips;
you plunged your nose into their scent,
there in the noisy TV room.
Your pleasure burst the glass in my heart
and let me glory in your joy.

Requiem

The day we buried my young nephew,
I went to sing the Verdi mass that thunders out
a "Dies irae," an ancient hymn of wrath intoned
in medieval naves and in my childhood church.

That afternoon, the music took my grief,
steeped it in fear, lifted it,
and set it down to rest at last.

The church where I grew up is made
from Pennsylvania field stone.
A painted wooden panel, red and lapis blue, rears above the altar.
On it, Christ crucified wears a golden halo.
A verse inscribed above him reads
Caro Cibus. Sanguis Potus.
        Eat my flesh, drink my blood.
This my young eyes feasted on.

In Florence once, a tinted burial scene
caught my eye—the sunken cheeks,
the long body shrouded in linen drapery.
In death, my mother, paper thin,
lay in cadaver like a fresco,
her mouth a fine blue line.

Would that we had sung her off with songs
she feared: *day of wrath, day of mourning,*
holy chants that lead us back
through flagellants and incense smoke
to an ancient flowing grief
larger than our single selves.

Still, I see her body lowered
in gold and medieval red
into the grave, the last station—

        her descent into the open earth, glistening.

Bone-House

In Old English, the human body is called a bone-house. The 4th century scholar, St. Jerome, is often depicted with a human cranium on his desk.

Saint Jerome ponders an ancient skull, polished
like a vase. Something to symbolize mortality.
But after many years, doesn't the skull become
familiar? An artifact lying around, keeping him company?
Does he ever scrub his thumb across the jagged edges of the
  nose,
or does he just pat the thing, admire the way
its curves resemble a water jug?
If death is your familiar, doesn't it lose its sting?

In the bath at night, I wash my head,
pressing my palm into the meager scalp.
My hair, gone years ago, left but an inch of flesh
between my hands and the immortal bone.
Long after everything that makes me
quirky and unrealized has vanished,
this cap of bone will still survive—
in a coffin most likely, cushioned against some pink sateen.
Maybe I should say good-bye to my too-hard head right now.

It's flesh I fancy. My middle fingers
warm the empty hollows
of my face; I lick my ever-peeling lips.
Oh lost and lingering flesh! Arms, nose,
cartilage—all like spirit, fade.
I am part of it, my flesh;
my cheeks and eyes and hips are me.
The bone, some distant stranger.

Author's Note on Lamellar Ichthyosis

The skin disorder with which I was born, called lamellar ichthyosis, is caused by a genetic abnormality. As a newborn, I was a "collodion baby," covered with a clear, shellac-like membrane that soon broke apart. Lamellar, or plate-like, ichthyosis manifests in heavy scaling, and in my case, a reddish hue to the skin. The build-up of scale is due to the fact that skin cells do not separate normally at the surface of the outermost layer of the skin and are not shed as quickly as they should be. In some cases, as in mine, the skin around the eyes pulls so tightly it causes the eyelids to turn outward, exposing the inner red lid.

Since 1982, I have benefitted from taking retinoids, a synthetic derivative of Vitamin A. This medicine, which I take in the form of yellow pills every morning, has greatly reduced the scales on my body.

More information is available at www.firstskinfoundation.org.

Acknowledgements

My thanks to the poets and writers who have encouraged me over the years and have edited these poems: Tina Barr, Catherine Carter, Alexandra Grilikhes, Ona Gritz, Stephen A. Kuusisto, Samantha Martin, Janet McAdams, Kate Millett, Minnie Bruce Pratt, Elaine Terranova, J.C. Todd, and Richard Wertime.

Thanks to Leonard Milstone, MD, of Yale University for years of encouragement and for checking my descriptions of ichthyosis.

Thanks also to the editors of the books and journals where the following poems first appeared, some in different versions.

American Writing: A Magazine: "Mother Love"
Apiary: "So Why Do Pain and Fear Buy Heaven?"
Amusejanetmason.com: "In Church"
Badlands: "Redlight Blue;" "In the Pink"
Beauty is a Verb: The New Poetry of Disability, ed. Sheila Black, Jennifer Bartlett and Michael Northen: "Cossetted"; "The Dermatological Society Skin Fair" in a version called "The Examining Table"
The Bucks County Writer: "You Would Understand How"
EOAGH: "Skull"
Harrington Lesbian Fiction Quarterly: "Debbie: Sunday Night Lover" in a slightly different version
Journal of Investigative Dermatology: "Heat"
Mad Poets Review: "Haven"
Muse apprentice guild: "The Dressing Table"
Philadelphia Poets: "All Souls'"; "The Bride Triumphant"; "Donkeys on Parade"; "Old Roses"; "My Mother's Voice"; "Requiem"
Schuylkill Valley Journal of the Arts: "Portrait"
Referential: "Bone-House"
Wordgathering: "A Clutch of Narcissus"; "Collodion Baby" in a version called "Forgiveness"